A-26 / B-26 Invade

In Action®

Written by David Doyle

Color Art by Don Greer

Line Illustrations by Todd Sturgell

Squadron Signal®
Publications

(Front Cover) Conceived before the United States entered WWII, the Douglas A-26 Invader provided Allied forces with a strike aircraft for that war, Korea, and even into the Vietnam War. The aircraft entered service with the Army Air Forces in 1943 and was retired by the U.S. Air Force in 1969. (National Museum of the United States Air Force)

(Back Cover) Douglas A-26B-50-DL (USAF serial number) 44-34230 assigned to the 13th Bombardment Squadron, 3rd Bombardment Group in Korea is painted overall in black in accordance with its role as a nighttime interdiction aircraft. It is equipped with a six-machine-gun nose and three machine guns in each wing. (Stan Piet collection)

About the In Action® Series

In Action® books, despite the title of the genre, are books that trace the development of a single type of aircraft, armored vehicle, or ship from prototype to the final production variant. Experimental or "one-off" variants can also be included. Our first *In Action®* book was printed in 1971.

ISBN 978-0-89747-818-2

Proudly printed in the U.S.A.
Copyright 2016 Squadron/Signal Publications
1115 Crowley Drive, Carrollton, TX 75006-1312 U.S.A.

Military/Combat Photographs and Snapshots

If you have any photos of aircraft, armor, soldiers, or ships of any nation, particularly wartime snapshots, please share them with us and help make Squadron/Signal's books all the more interesting and complete in the future. Any photograph sent to us will be copied and returned as requested. Electronic images are preferred. The donor will be fully credited for any photos used. Please send them to:

Squadron/Signal Publications
1115 Crowley Drive
Carrollton, TX 75006-1312 U.S.A.
www.SquadronSignalPublications.com

(Title Page) The A-26/B-26 Invader served with distinction and versatility as an attack bomber from World War II to Korea and Vietnam. A-26B-61-DL 44-34548 has been converted to A-26C standards with the installation of a clear bombardier's nose and painted black. (Stan Piet collection)

Acknowledgments

Few non-fiction books can be written as a solo effort, and this volume is no exception. While my name appears on the cover, it would have been impossible to assemble with a great deal of help from my friends. The assistance of these individuals and institutions cannot be overstated: Tom Kailbourn, Scott Taylor, Dana Bell, Stan Piet, Brett Stolle at the National Museum of the United States Air Force (NMUSAF), the staff of the U.S. National Archives, and the editorial team at Squadron-Signal Publications. Most of all, the support and help of my wonderful wife Denise made this book possible.

Introduction

Only one month after the Douglas A-20 flew for the first time, the company's chief engineer Ed Heinemann, along with Robert Donovan, began work on a new aircraft design that they intended to replace not only their A-20, but also the North American B-25 and Martin B-26.

Drawing on experiences gleaned with the DB-7, the export aircraft from which the A-20 was derived, Douglas engineers fashioned an attack bomber with increased defensive armament, increased bomb load, more power and the potential for either a transparent or a gun nose.

While the U.S. military provided input on the new design, the effort was a Douglas-initiated project. This initiative gave the company considerable latitude in design, rather than striving to meet specified goals and characteristics. The company completed a full-size wooden mockup, which was shown to Army Air Corps representatives on 11-12 April 1941.

The military was sufficiently impressed to issue contract W-535-AC-17946 on 2 June 1941 to develop the design further. The initial contract value was $2,083,385.79, plus a fee of slightly more than $125,000. By the end of the month the contract had been amended to include a third prototype.

Thus began the production of the A-26, which was quickly dubbed the Invader. Various delays left the first production aircraft in the Douglas assembly line until September 1943. Even once production began, deliveries lagged and led a frustrated General Hap Arnold to write, "One thing is certain: I want the A-26s for use in this war and not for the next war. If something drastic is not done we cannot hope to replace the B-25s, B-26s and A-20s with the A-26."

Ultimately General Arnold did get his A-26s for use in WWII, but they were also used not only in "the next" war (Korea), but also the one after that (Vietnam). They finally retired in 1969.

The response to the early combat operations of the A-26 provided no more encouragement than the struggles with production. Far East Air Forces commander General George C. Kenney remarked, "We do not want the A-26 under any circumstances as a replacement for anything."

The Invader, and a skilled crew, proved its merit. Later, even General Kenney note, "...the version with the eight-gun nose and no bottom turret had proved to be highly satisfactory as a replacement for the A-20s and B-25s."

It was designed with ease of maintenance as a consideration. It also had impressive armaments, which included a 6,000-pound bomb load, up to 14 forward-firing machine guns. Late-production aircraft had a 2,000-gallon fuel capacity to yield impressive range and loiter times. The Invader lived up to the expectations of Douglas and the military.

These characteristics led the Invader to be retained after WWII, a time when many aircraft were phased out, and to advance to fight again not only in Korea, but also in Vietnam. It was flown first by the French in the 1950s in Vietnam, and also by the U.S. Air Force until 1969.

The A-26 Invader was a Douglas company-initiated project. The project's intent was to replace the North American B-25 Mitchell, Martin B-26 Marauder, and this aircraft, the Douglas A-20 Havoc, with a single airplane. The A-26 bears more than a passing resemblance to its predecessor the A-20. This is expected since many of the same designers and engineers worked on both projects.

When Douglas first proposed the A-26 to the Army Air Forces, the proposal included the XA-26A, a night fighter version. The A-26A was a continuation of the A-20-derived P-70, such as this example dubbed *Black Magic.* Because the Northrop P-61 Black Widow (background) advanced development, no further effort was put into the XA-26A. The A-26A designation was revived for the production gun-nose version of the Invader.

The XA-26-DE flies over El Segundo in July 1942. It featured a clear bombardier's nose. With production of the its A-20 Havoc attack aircraft underway, Douglas Aircraft began the design and development of an advanced twin-engine attack aircraft. Edward Heinemann and Robert Donovan spearheaded the project. They wanted an aircraft that would combine the best traits of the Douglas A-20, the North American B-25, and the Martin B-26. Douglas produced three prototype aircraft with varying roles and noses at its El Segundo, California, plant. The DE suffix stood for Douglas, El Segundo. (National Museum of the United States Air Force (NMUSAF)

Although the War Department had issued Douglas contracts for three examples of the new attack bomber, all three were to be different and designated XA-26-DE. The first of the experimental versions was to be configured as a three-seat attack bomber. As such, the aircraft was to feature a transparent nose with provision for a bombardier. The DE suffix of the model designation indicated that the prototype aircraft was to be built by the Douglas El Segundo, California plant.

The first flight of the aircraft was pushed from 15 January 1942 to 1 July. The inability to secure needed components resulted from war production and rationing. Specifically cited were the lack of landing gear struts, self-sealing fuel tanks, turrets and Government Furnished Equipment, which included the two Pratt & Whitney R-2800-27 radial engines and associated propellers. It is not unusual for certain components in military contracts to be procured by the government and furnished to a contractor for inclusion in a larger item. This arrangement was often the case with engines and propellers on military aircraft. Not only did it make the component manufacturer directly accountable to the government, but it sometimes lowered the finished item cost.

The initial flight of the XA-26-DE 41-19504 ultimately took place on 10 July 1942. Douglas test pilot Ben O. Howard was at the controls while various Douglas and Army Air Corps personnel watched.

The XA-26 prototype was rolled out of the El Segundo plant in June 1942, and taxi tests began shortly thereafter. Test pilot Howard, upon landing the XA-26, was enthusiastic about the performance of the aircraft, whose first flight had been uneventful.

The clear nose of the XA-26-DE was similar to the production A-26C. However, an aluminum cheek protruded into the lower right part of the nose. This protrusion was part of a proposed twin, fixed-machine-gun mount. A test probe was installed on the nose. (NMUSAF)

All three prototypes, which included this XA-26-DE, were armed with dorsal and ventral turrets. Each turret had two .50-caliber machine guns. A gunner was stationed to the rear of the bomb bay, and he controlled both turrets remotely. The gunner had a clear top to the rear of the dorsal turret. Periscopes helped the gunner aim the guns at targets. Although the tail number was 219504, the actual USAAF serial number was 41-19504. (NMUSAF)

XA-26-DE, the first prototype, conducts a test flight. The aluminum cheek that normally protrudes into the right side of the lower half of the clear bombardier's nose was not present on the left side of the nose. The large spinners on the propellers interfered with engine cooling and eventually were removed. (NMUSAF)

The XA-26-DE, like the other two prototypes and the production A-26s, had laminar-flow wings. The airfoil was symmetrical with the same curvature on the top and bottom of laminar-flow wing surfaces. Also, the chord of the wing was designed to be at its thickest as far aft as possible. Laminar-flow wings were designed to reduce air turbulence on the wings. They also resulted in lower drag. (National Archives)

XA-26A-DE was the second prototype produced by Douglas. It was configured as a night-fighter. The nose featured a centimetric MIT AI-4 radar housed in a radome. The armament consisted of four 20mm cannons in a gondola under the bomb bay with ammunition stored inside the bay. The ventral turret was eliminated while the dorsal turret had four .50-caliber machine guns. (NMUSAF)

The second prototype aircraft in the 2 June contract was designated the XA-26A-DE. Also built in El Segundo, this aircraft was configured as a night fighter. The aircraft was envisioned as a competitor to the Northrop P-61 Black Widow. It was armed with four 20mm cannons housed in a large blister beneath the fuselage. The dorsal turret sported four .50-caliber machine guns. The three-man crew of the XA-26A was to use the radar set to locate and home in on its prey. The radar antenna would be housed in and on the nose and wings of the aircraft. A radome would replace the transparent nose utilized on the XA-26.

The radar set was to be the SCR-540. It was the Western Electric-produced copy of the British Mark IV Airborne Intercept radar set, which was first tested the same month that the XA-26A contract was issued. This equipment provided the radar operator with two 3-inch cathode ray tubes, which displayed target azimuth and elevation.

While the forward bomb bay was to be used as an ammunition magazine for the belly-mounted 20mm cannons, the rear bomb bay could be used during night intruder missions. It could carry up to 2,000 pounds in bombs. One likely reason that the XA-26A retained the attack bomber designation, unlike the similarly reader-equipped variant of the A-20 (the P-70), was to function as a bomber, albeit with a reduced bomb load.

The prototype XA-26A 41-19505 was to be the sole example of the type. Production of the Black Widow was underway, and USAAF officials believed the XA-26A offered no advantage.

The Douglas XA-26A-DE prototype night-fighter carried the tail number 119505, which was its USAAF serial number minus the first digit. A Plexiglas dome was installed on the gunner/radar operator's clear top enclosure, for improved all-around visibility. (NMUSAF)

The depth of the gondola for the four 20mm cannons under the Douglas XA-26A-DE fuselage is apparent. Despite the problems encountered with the propeller spinners on the XA-26-DE, the spinners were still on the XA-26A-DE during trials. The flat canopy top would be revised on the A-26B and A-26C productions. (NMUSAF)

Exhausts of the XA-26A-DE pilot night-fighter glow at night with combustion from the Pratt & Whitney R-2800-27 engines. The rear gondola contour is smooth for the 20mm cannons. (NMUSAF)

The Douglas XA-26A-DE runs up its engines during a night test in August 1944. The run-up of the engines helps identify the plane's characteristic exhaust flares. The exhausts were in groups of four around the perimeter of the cowl. (NMUSAF)

Light reflects off the left propeller of the XA-26A-DE as it moves. The propeller's virtual volume creates an illusion of a large bulge under the fuselage. The effect should not be mistaken for the cannon gondola. The tires have a diamond-tread pattern. (NMUSAF)

Flight tests were favorable for XA-26A-DE in August 1944. However, it was not put into production because the Army Air Forces opted instead for the Northrop P-61 Black Widow night fighter. (NMUSAF)

XA-26B-DE 41-19588 was the third prototype that resulted from Ed Heinemann's and Robert Donovan's project to develop a twin-engine advanced attack aircraft. It was intended as a solid-nosed attack aircraft. A 75mm cannon protruded from the right side of the nose. The pilot and the cannoneer/navigator sat in the cockpit while the gunner operated the dorsal and ventral turrets in the rear. (NMUSAF)

Only three weeks after the contract for the experimental XA-26 and XA-26A was awarded, a third experimental variant was ordered. Designated XA-26B, this model featured a solid, or unglazed, nose to house a 75mm cannon.

Three men were to crew the aircraft. The navigator was also the cannon loader and sat beside the pilot in the cockpit. The third crewman was positioned behind the wings, and controlled both the dorsal and ventral turrets. The gun turrets were operated by remote control.

A fourth seat was provided behind the navigator's position for passengers or observers.

The big 75mm cannon installation was also tried in the North American B-25, but just as with the North American aircraft, other armament combinations were considered as well.

By September 1942 another weapons installations consideration included a nose with four 37mm guns and/or two 37mm guns mounted beneath the bomb bay. Shortly thereafter, plans were drawn for various combinations of .50-caliber machine gun and 37mm plus 75mm cannon armament.

As orders poured into Douglas for its Navy dive bomber, the El Segundo-built SBD Dauntless, and its Army equivalent, the A-24, it became clear that the facility could not handle A-26 production as well. Thus, XA-26B-DE 41-19588 was the final A-26 built in El Segundo.

The 75mm cannon barrel of the XA-26B-DE protrudes from a faired recess on the lower right of the solid nose. The muzzle of the cannon was fitted with a clamshell-type cover to streamline the barrel and prevent foreign objects from entering the muzzle. (NMUSAF)

The Douglas XA-26B-DE right side displays its 75mm cannon barrel on 24 May 1943. The top periscope head for the turret gunner's optical sight system is on the clear cover over the gunner's compartment. The lower periscope head is on the bottom of the fuselage directly below the top periscope. The tail number, 219588, is in small numerals on the vertical tail. (NMUSAF)

The clamshell cover of the 75mm cannon in the XA-26B-DE is shown in the retracted position, with the muzzle of the gun cleared to fire. It was projected that the XA-26B-DE's solid nose could also contain other configurations of weapons. (NMUSAF)

The clamshell cover for the 75mm gun muzzle is here retracted on the nose of the XA-26B-DE. The faired recess in the nose for the gun barrel was similar in idea to the ones used on the 75mm-gun-equipped North American B-25G and B-25H. (NMUSAF)

The stance of the XA-26B-DE on its tricycle landing gear is evident on 24 May 1944. The dihedral of the wings is apparent. For production A-26s, the dihedral was 4.5 degrees, and it was the same for the XA-26B-DE. Ram scoops for the carburetors were on the upper fronts of the anti-drag rings of the cowlings. On the wings outboard of the nacelles were air scoops for the oil coolers. (NMUSAF)

From this angle, the bullet-shaped clamshell-door cover of the XA-26B-DE's 75mm gun remains visible. A protrusion is atop the roof of the cockpit to the rear of the pilot's seat. This feature has a flat front with an opening at the top and a curved rear. Although the purpose of this feature is uncertain, it may have housed a periscopic sight for the cannon. (NMUSAF)

Modifications were later implemented on the XA-26B-DE. The 75mm cannon has been removed, and a port in the nose was covered. The protrusion on the left side of the cockpit roof was removed. The propeller spinners have been omitted to improve engine cooling. Also, the plane had been repainted. (National Archives)

A-26 / B-26 Development

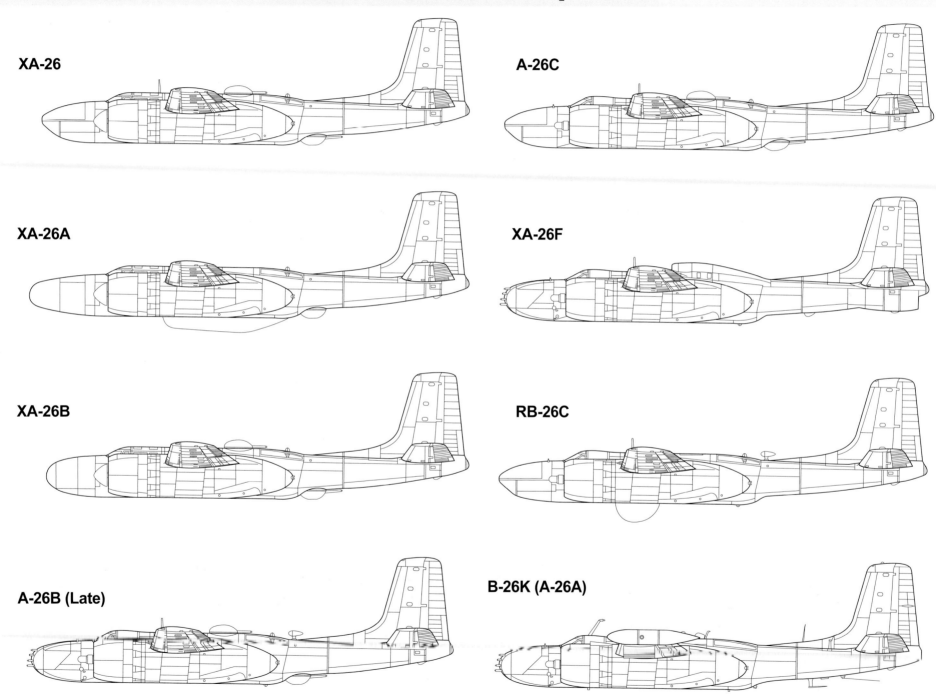

XA-26

XA-26A

XA-26B

A-26B (Late)

A-26C

XA-26F

RB-26C

B-26K (A-26A)

After the successful tests of the XA-26 prototypes, series production commenced on the A-26B. A-26B-1-DL 41-39108 is the ninth plane from the first production block. The DL suffix stood for Douglas Aircraft's Long Beach, California plant. The original plan was for the A-26B to have a variety of nose-armament options, such as this 75mm cannon. (NMUSAF)

Even before the first Invader took to the air, a contract for 500 production A-26s had been awarded. Dated in October 1941, the contract was modified several times. After the program was repeatedly delayed by material, tooling and component shortages, production of the A-26B finally began with the first six production models being built with the prototype tooling.

Like the XA-26B, the B-26B featured a solid rather than transparent nose. After considerable debate, the armament arrangement was changed. The 75mm-armed version, which had been a priority into the summer of 1942, was not to be built. Instead, the nose would house six .50-caliber machine guns. The original plans had called for the nose assembly of the aircraft to be easily interchangeable, and that feature was retained. Thus later when eight-gun noses were introduced, they were readily installed on older aircraft, as were clear noses from the A-26C and vice-versa.

Underwing provisions of the early aircraft allowed up to two fixed twin .50-caliber machine gun pods to be mounted underneath each wing outboard of the nacelle. Ammunition stowage was in the wing. Due to drag, later production A-26Bs lacked this feature, instead having three .50-caliber machine guns mounted internally in each wing.

Another change made during production involved the engine. Initially powered by the R-2800-27 or R-2800-71, the water-injected R-2800-79 was adopted after 700 were built. Original plans also called for the A-26B to be built at Long Beach and Tulsa, but after 205 Tulsa-built had been completed it was decided to concentrate A-26C production in the Oklahoma plant. This left Long Beach the sole source for the A-26B. Long Beach produced 1,150 A-26B aircraft before production was stopped on 27 August 1945.

A-26B-10-DL 41-39136 displays markings for the 553rd Bombardment Squadron, 386th Bombardment Group in 1944. These markings include the code "AN" on the fuselage and a yellow band edged in black on the vertical tail. A radio-direction-finder (RDF) loop antenna is on the rear deck. (National Archives)

A Douglas A-20, left, and a Douglas A-26 are parked side by side for the purpose of this comparative view. Noticeable differences between the two aircraft include the more squared fuselage top of the A-26; the less-rounded tips of the A-26's vertical tail, horizontal stabilizer, and wings; the glazed dorsal turret of the A-20 versus the solid-domed, remote-control turret of the A-26, and the wider wingspan of the A-26. (National Archives)

A-26B-10-DL 41-39136 has a plain nose with no armaments. The A-26B's all-purpose nose was adaptable to different armaments. The number 37 is marked on the side of the nose. Antiglare panels are on the nacelles. (National Archives)

Douglas A-26B-10-DL 41-39136, configured with an all-purpose nose with no armaments installed, is viewed from the front right during a test flight over the Southern California desert. The panel lines of the nose assembly are discernible.

Douglas A-26B-10-DL 41-39136 now has a battery of six .50-caliber machine guns installed in the nose. Four guns are arranged on the right half of the nose and two are on the left half. Early on, A-26Bs also had the option to carry one or two twin-.50-caliber package guns under each wing for extra firepower. The dorsal and the ventral turrets are present. (National Archives)

A-26B-10-DL 41-39136 displays its configuration with six nose-mounted .50-caliber machine guns. For this part of the experiments with different nose configurations, the ventral turret has been removed and faired over. The shapes of the bomb-bay doors are apparent from this angle. (National Archives)

An A-26B armament suite in the nose consists of a T13E1 75mm cannon on the right side and two Browning M2 .50-caliber machine guns on the left side. Unlike the 75mm cannon installation on the XA-26B, this cannon was not fitted with a clamshell cover. A small opening was on the very point of the nose. The opening was for the gun camera. The pilot aimed these guns with an N9 gun sight or a ring-and-bead sight. (National Archives)

This B-26B, as the A-26B was redesignated in 1948, is configured with eight .50-caliber M2 machine guns in the nose and two twin .50-caliber gun packages under each wing. The nose guns were arranged in two vertical rows of four guns each. The package guns were mounted in fairings attached to special hangers that were screwed to the undersides of the wings. The guns were fed from ammunition boxes inside the wings. (NMUSAF)

The machine guns in the six-gun nose configuration of A-26B-10-DL 41-39136 were staggered. The two center guns protrude the farthest to the front. The canopy frame of the early A-26s was extremely cumbersome. This canopy design resulted in reduced visibility from the cockpit. Soon, this problem would be remedied by a new canopy with a bulged top and thinner frame members. (National Archives)

Two package guns are mounted on a B-26B in 1953. At the bottom center of each package-gun fairing were two cartridge-ejector chutes, one in front of the other. On each side of the bottom of the fairings were smaller chutes to eject ammunition links. On the front end of the bottom of each fairing were two access panels for the fairing-mounting bolts. There were two similar panels for the rear mounting bolts. (NMUSAF)

Early A-26Bs had six .50-caliber machine guns in the nose. Later, an eight-gun nose became the norm. Optional armament includes other groups of nose armaments - both considered or realized - for the A-26B. Groups feature mixtures of .50-caliber, 37mm, and 75mm guns.

Standard Armament

Optional Armament

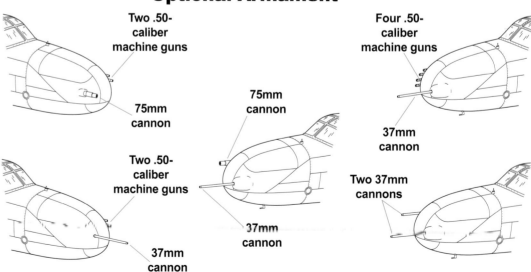

A-26B (early) — Six .50-caliber machine guns

A-26B (late) — Eight .50-caliber machine guns

Two .50-caliber machine guns
75mm cannon

Two .50-caliber machine guns
37mm cannon

75mm cannon
37mm cannon

Four .50-caliber machine guns
37mm cannon
Two 37mm cannons

Invader Serial Numbers and Production Blocks

Invader production was spread among three Douglas plants during WWII. This production was divided into blocks or small groups of aircraft within each model. Most changes in production coincided with changes in block number. Standardization of the clamshell canopy with the A-26B-30-DL block is one example. As in this example, the block numbers (-30) were appended to the aircraft model number, while the suffix (-DL for Long Beach, -DT for Tulsa, and -DE for El Segundo) followed the block number. This table includes orders, by the Army Air Forces, and the USAF, as well as A-26 production serial numbers and block numbers, which include the remanufacturing of Invaders by On Mark Engineering.

Serial Number	Block
Prototypes	
41-19504	XA-26-DE
41-19505	XA-26A-DE
41-19588	XA-26B-DE
A-26B	
41-39100 – 41-39104	A-26B-1-DL
41-39105 – 41-39119	A-26B-5-DL
41-39120 – 41-39139	A-26B-10-DL
41-39140 – 41-39151	A-26B-15-DL
41-39153 – 41-39192	A-26B-15-DL
41-39194	A-26B-15-DL
41-39196 – 41-39198	A-26B-15-DL
41-39201 – 41-39299	A-26B-20-DL
41-39300 – 41-39349	A-26B-25-DL
41-39350 – 41-39424	A-26B-30-DL
41-39425 – 41-39499	A-26B-35-DL
41-39500 – 41-39599	A-26B-40-DL
43-22252 – 43-22266	A-26B-5-DT
43-22267 – 43-22301	A-26B-10-DT
43-22302 – 43-22303	A-26B-16-DT
43-22305 – 43-22307	A-26B-15-DT

Serial Number	Block
43-22313 – 43-22345	A-26B-15-DT
43-22350 – 43-22399	A-26B-15-DT
43-22400 – 43-22453	A-26B-20-DT
43-22454 – 43-22466	A-26B-25-DT
44-34098 – 44-34217	A-26B-45-DL
44-34218 – 44-34286	A-26B-50-DL
44-34287	A-26B-51-DL
44-34288 – 44-34296	A-26B-50-DL
44-34297 – 44-34298	A-26B-51-DL
44-34299 – 44-34322	A-26B-50-DL
44-34323	A-26B-51-DL
44-34324 – 44-34326	A-26B-50-DL
44-34327	A-26B-51-DL
44-34328 – 44-34330	A-26B-50-DL
44-34331	A-26B-51-DL
44-34332	A-26B-50-DL
44-34333 – 44-34334	A-26B-55-DL
44-34335	A-26B-56-DL
44-34336 – 44-34338	A-26B-55-DL
44-34339	A-26B-56-DL
44-34340 – 44-34342	A-26B-55-DL
44-34343	A-26B-56-DL
44-34344 – 44-34346	A-26B-55-DL
44-34347	A-26B-56-DL
44-34348 – 44-34350	A-26B-55-DL
44-34351	A-26B-56-DL
44-34352 – 44-34363	A-26B-55-DL
44-34364	A-26B-56-DL
44-34365 – 44-34367	A-26B-55-DL
44-34368	A-26B-56-DL
44-34369 – 44-34371	A-26B-55-DL
44-34372	A-26B-56-DL
44-34373 – 44-34376	A-26B-55-DL
44-34377	A-26B-56-DL
44-34378 – 44-34381	A-26B-55-DL
44-34382	A-26B-56-DL
44-34383 – 44-34386	A-26B-55-DL
44-34387	A-26B-56-DL
44-34388 – 44-34392	A-26B-55-DL
44-34393	A-26B-56-DL
44-34394 – 44-34398	A-26B-55-DL

Serial Number	Block
44-34399	A-26B-56-DL
44-34400 – 44-34404	A-26B-55-DL
44-34405	A-26B-56-DL
44-34406 – 44-34408	A-26B-55-DL
44-34409	A-26B-56-DL
44-34410 – 44-34412	A-26B-55-DL
44-34413	A-26B-56-DL
44-34414 – 44-34416	A-26B-55-DL
44-34417	A-26B-56-DL
44-34418 – 44-34419	A-26B-55-DL
44-34420	A-26B-56-DL
44-34421 – 44-34422	A-26B-55-DL
44-34423	A-26B-56-DL
44-34424 – 44-34472	A-26B-55-DL
44-34473 – 44-34477	A-26B-60-DL
44-34478	A-26B-61-DL
44-34479 – 44-34480	A-26B-60-DL
44-34481	A-26B-61-DL
44-34482 – 44-34483	A-26B-60-DL
44-34484	A-26B-61-DL
44-34485 – 44-34486	A-26B-60-DL
44-34487	A-26B-61-DL
44-34488 – 44-34489	A-26B-60-DL
44-34490	A-26B-61-DL
44-34491 – 44-34492	A-26B-60-DL
44-34493	A-26B-61-DL
44-34494 – 44-34495	A-26B-60-DL
44-34496	A-26B-61-DL
44-34497 – 44-34498	A-26B-60-DL
44-34499	A-26B-61-DL
44-34500 – 44-34501	A-26B-60-DL
44-34502	A-26B-61-DL
44-34503 – 44-34504	A-26B-60-DL
44-34505	A-26B-61-DL
44-34506 – 44-34507	A-26B-60-DL
44-34508	A-26B-61-DL
44-34509 – 44-34510	A-26B-60-DL
44-34511	A-26B-61-DL
44-34512 – 44-34513	A-26B-60-DL
44-34514	A-26B-61-DL
44-34515 – 44-34516	A-26B-60-DL

Serial Number	Block
44-34517	A-26B-61-DL
44-34518 – 44-34519	A-26B-60-DL
44-34520	A-26B-61-DL
44-34521	A-26B-60-DL
44-34522 – 44-34585	A-26B-61-DL
44-34587 – 44-34617	A-26B-61-DL
44-34618 – 44-34753	A-26B-66-DL
A-26C	
41-39152	A-26C-1-DL
41-39193	A-26C-2-DL
41-39195	A-26C-2-DL
41-39199 – 41-39200	A-26C-2-DL
43-22304	A-26C-16-DT
43-22308 – 43-22312	A-26C-16-DT
43-22346 – 43-22349	A-26C-16-DT
43-22467 – 43-22493	A-26C-15-DT
43-22494 – 43-22564	A-26C-20-DT
43-22565 – 43-22751	A-26C-25-DT
44-35198 – 44-35357	A-26C-30-DT
44-35358 – 44-35557	A-26C-35-DT
44-35558 – 44-35562	A-26C-40-DT
44-35564 – 44-35655	A-26C-40-DT
44-35656 – 44-35782	A-26C-45-DT
44-35783 – 44-35937	A-26C-50-DT
44-35938 – 44-35947	A-26C-55-DT
44-35953	A-26C-55-DT
44-35955	A-26C-55-DT
44-35957 – 44-35996	A-26C-55-DT
XA-26D	
44-34776	XA-26D-DL
XA-26E	
44-35563	XA-26E-DL
XA-26F	
44-34586	XA-26F-DL
B-26K (A-26A) Counter Invader	
64-17640 – 64-17679	On Mark B-26K

This early A-26B has the early-type cockpit canopy. This style of canopy had a fixed roof over the pilot's side of the cockpit. It also featured a front-hinged hatch with a heavy frame and two windows in it above the right side of the cockpit. This was the only hatch available to the pilot if a bailout was necessary. It was in a difficult position for him to negotiate. (National Archives)

This A-26B, armed with six .50-caliber machine guns in the nose in addition to turret guns, is equipped with two clamshell doors in the canopy enclosure over the cockpit. These canopy doors had thin frames and curved Plexiglas windows. They were hinged on the bottom edges and provided better visibility and means of egress for the pilot. (National Archives)

A-26B-20-DL 41-39245 features the pilot's clamshell door with a bulged top. A triangular vent panel is located toward the rear of the door. A vent panel is on the windscreen. Mounted above the windscreen is a blind-landing antenna. (National Archives)

The turret gunner's top periscope head is visible in England in 1944. The gunner sighted through a top and a bottom periscope with a 70 degree field of view. It is modified with a wire gadget for the gunner to establish aim and kill zones. (National Archives)

The dorsal turret enclosure of an A-26B is removed. The .50-caliber machine guns are mounted and point toward the empennage. The turret was a General Electric product. A fire interrupter assembly prevented guns from firing into the wing, tail and propellers. The clear enclosure for the gunner has unusual small blisters on each side. (NMUSAF)

The enclosure of an A-26B ventral turret is removed. The Browning .50-caliber M2 machine-gun installation is mounted. Both turrets had 360 degree traverse, with a maximum electronic slew speed of 45 degrees per second in traverse and 30 in elevation. (NMUSAF)

The gunner's control station consisted of periscopic sights and manual controls linked to a central fire-control system. The central fire-control system regulated the aim and fire of the guns in the two turrets. The gunner's eyepiece and cushioned head rest are at the top of the structure. (NMUSAF)

Douglas A-26B-20-DL 41-39264 flies over Dallas in 1945. This plane's all-purpose nose was armed with six .50-caliber machine guns. The canopy is the clamshell type. Stripes indicate walkways on the inboard halves of the wings. (National Archives)

Douglas A-26B-20-DL 41-39264 cruises near Dallas in 1945. Behind the cockpit are the antenna mast and an angled stub antenna. Under the fuselage and below the cockpit is the retractable boarding ladder, which someone neglected to retract. (National Archives)

On the left side of the A-26B cockpit are control panels for systems such as the fire extinguisher, heaters, recognition lights, and communications. Toward the front of the left side is the electrical distribution panel. To the right are the control column and yoke. (NMUSAF)

On the pedestal to the right of the pilot's seat are the throttle and fuel-mixture control levers, the propeller controls, the landing-gear control lever, emergency brake lever, flap controls, and more. On the rear, lower part of the console are three fuel selector valves. (NMUSAF)

A special instrument panel is seen to the right of the main instrument panel in the cockpit of an A-26B on 10 October 1946. It includes pairs of torquemeters, tachometers, and several other gauges. The pedestal is at the bottom. (NMUSAF)

Several designs of cockpit canopies were employed on A-26s. For example, Douglas A-26B-25-DL 41-39322 exhibits a right clamshell door. The wrap-around windows terminated well above the bottom of the door's frame.

The bomb-bay doors are open on A-26B-35-DL 41-39456 during a flight on 27 February 1945. The three vertical slats immediately to the front of the bomb bay were retractable bomb-bay spoilers. They rested in a slot in the bottom of the fuselage during flight. Immediately before the bomb-bay doors open, the spoilers were hydraulically lowered to interrupt the flow of air into the bomb bay. This action increased air stability when the bombs were released. (National Archives)

A-26B Invader Nose Development

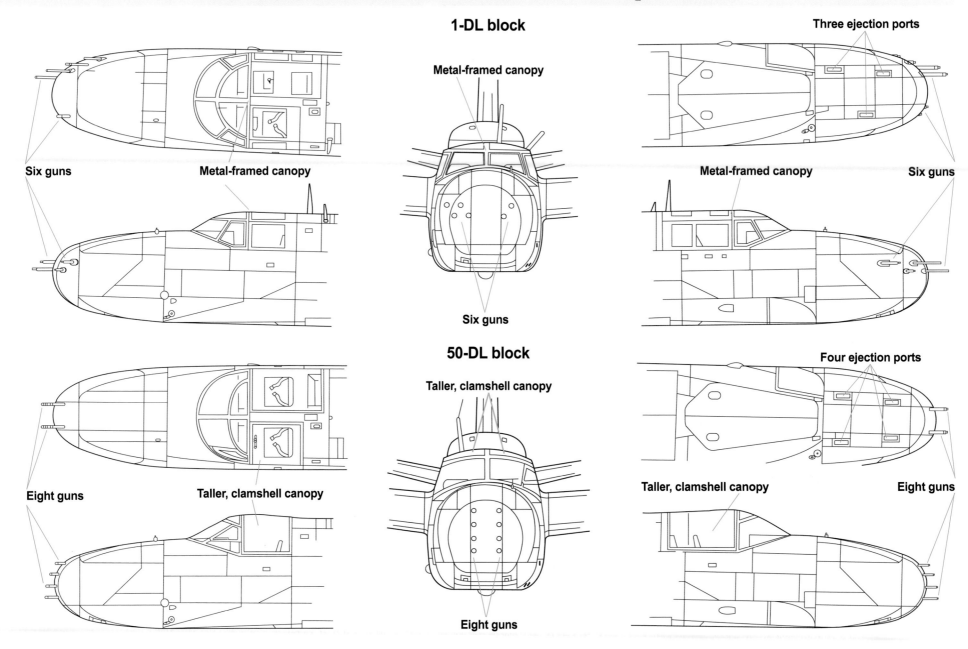

1-DL block

Metal-framed canopy

Three ejection ports

Six guns

Metal-framed canopy

Metal-framed canopy

Six guns

Six guns

50-DL block

Taller, clamshell canopy

Four ejection ports

Eight guns

Taller, clamshell canopy

Taller, clamshell canopy

Eight guns

Eight guns

These illustrations show the differences between the nose of an initial production gun-nose Invader, A-26B-1-DL, and a late production, block A-26-50-DL, aircraft. The A-26B-1-DL features a six-gun nose and early cockpit canopy. The A-26B-50-DL features an eight-gun nose and clamshell canopy.

Eight-Gun Nose

Port view

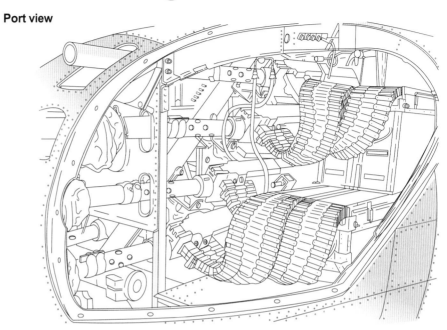

Starboard view

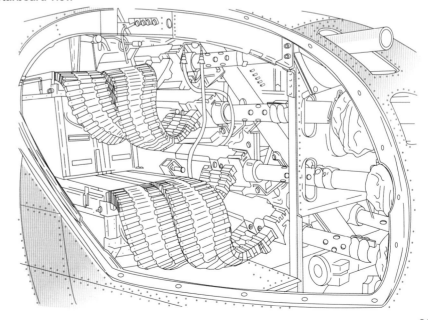

An A-26B features an eight-gun installation of Browning .50-caliber M2 machine guns in an all-purpose nose in Korea in 1953. The guns were in two vertical rows aligned one above the next. Blast tubes were frequently installed over the gun barrels to conceal the perforated cooling jackets of the barrels. (National Archives)

Right: These illustrations depict the left (port) and the right (starboard) sides of the interior of the A-26B's all-purpose nose with an installation of eight .50-caliber machine guns. Removable panels on the sides of the nose allowed easy and fast access to the guns, ammunition boxes, and flexible feed chutes. When the six-machine-gun configuration was installed in the all-purpose nose, the arrangements were different.

29

Douglas A-26B Invader

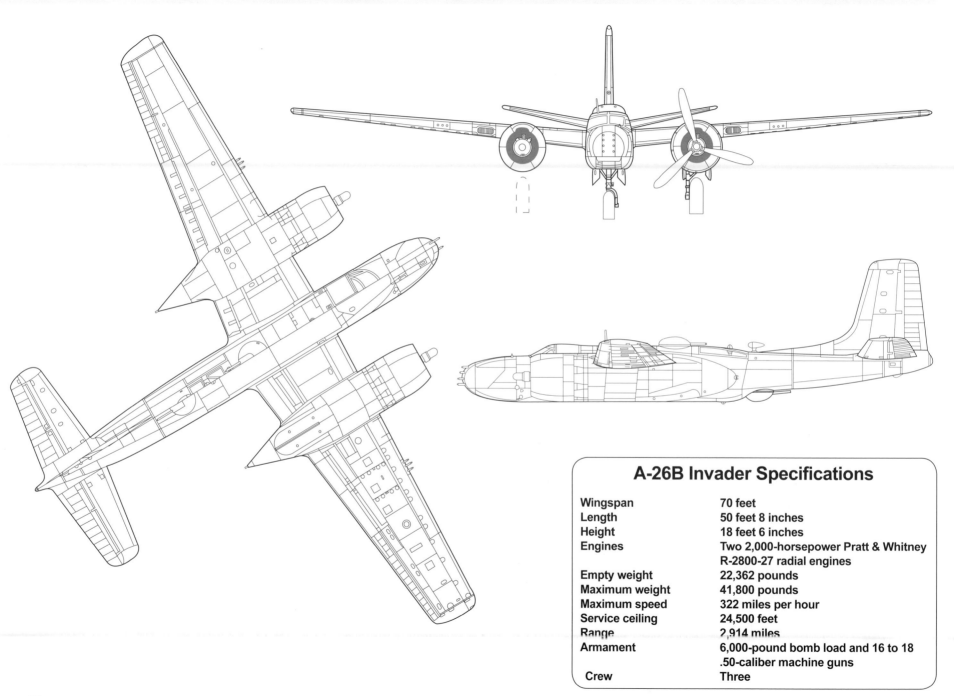

A-26B Invader Specifications

Wingspan	70 feet
Length	50 feet 8 inches
Height	18 feet 6 inches
Engines	Two 2,000-horsepower Pratt & Whitney R-2800-27 radial engines
Empty weight	22,362 pounds
Maximum weight	41,800 pounds
Maximum speed	322 miles per hour
Service ceiling	24,500 feet
Range	2,914 miles
Armament	6,000-pound bomb load and 16 to 18 .50-caliber machine guns
Crew	Three

The A-26C was produced concurrently with the A-26B. Their main difference was in the nose because the A-26C has a clear nose to accommodate a bombardier. Progressive upgrades made to the A-26B on the assembly line also were included in the A-26C. Two fixed .50-caliber machine guns were mounted in the right side of the A-26C nose. The small, staggered ports for these guns are visible. (NMUSAF)

Douglas A-26C-20-DT 43-22502 displays its original bare-aluminum finish. A radio-direction-finder (RDF) "football" antenna was mounted aft of the gunner's enclosure. Douglas' plant in Tulsa, Oklahoma, produced most A-26Cs (1,086) while Douglas' Long Beach, California, plant built far more A-26B planes. The Long Beach facility produced only five A-26Cs. (NMUSAF)

The A-26C was structurally identical to the A-26B. The exceptions were a transparent nose and pair of .50-caliber machine guns mounted on the right (starboard) side. Planners decided both the Long Beach and Tulsa plants would build the A-26C alongside the A-26B. Such production was quickly realized to be less efficient. After only five A-26Cs were built at Long Beach, it was decided that the A-26C models would thereafter be built exclusively in Tulsa while Long Beach concentrated on A-26Bs.

The A-26C was intended to serve as a lead ship for formations of A-26B aircraft while following aircraft released their bomb loads on the signal of the lead ship. By April 1945 USAAF requirements were such that the aircraft were produced in a ratio of one clear nose A-26C for every pair of gun-nose A-26B aircraft.

The various airframe production changes on the A-26B were also implemented on the A-26C. These changes included the clamshell-style canopy introduced at the A-26C-DT production block.

The A-26C-45-DT production block changes included water injection-equipped R-2800-79 engines, increased fuel capacity, underwing rockets, and three .50-caliber machine guns mounted in each wing.

Production of the A-26C began in early 1944 and stopped during June 1945 after 1,086 had left the Tulsa assembly line and an additional five examples were produced in Long Beach. Of these, 127 were modified by Douglas into the dual-control TA-26C trainer configuration.

The all-purpose nose of the late A-26B featured eight .50-caliber machine guns compared to the clear bombardier's nose of the A-236C. The clear nose had both an upper and lower component. The lower part held an flat panel of optical glass for the bomb sight.

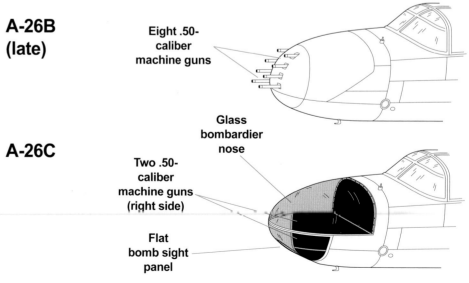

A-26B (late)

Eight .50-caliber machine guns

A-26C

Glass bombardier nose

Two .50-caliber machine guns (right side)

Flat bomb sight panel

A-26C-20-DT 43-22502 has the early-type cockpit enclosure with the flat top. The two machine-gun ports on the right side of the nose are visible. The clear bombardier's nose of the A-26C actually was interchangeable with the all-purpose gun nose. It was quite common to swap the noses. Power was provided by two Pratt & Whitney Double Wasp 18-cylinder R-2800-27 or R-2800-71 air-cooled, 2,000-horsepower radial engines. (NMUSAF)

The front of a late A-26C fuselage illustrates a bulged canopy and clamshell doors. The front perspective shows the angles of clamshell doors in the open positions.

A-26C

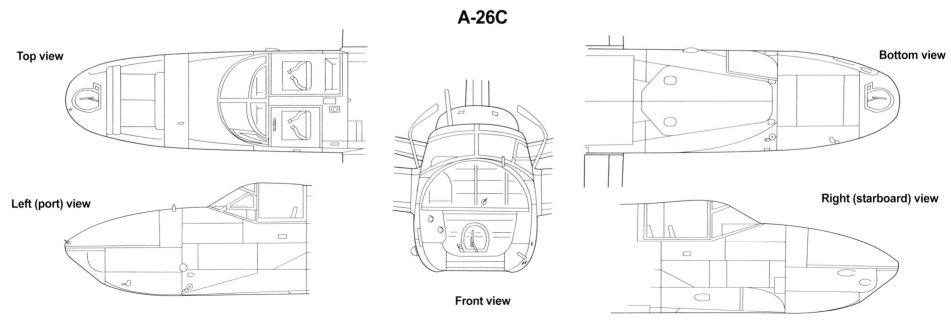

Top view

Left (port) view

Front view

Bottom view

Right (starboard) view

Douglas A-26C-20-DT 43-22502 is observed from the rear in a photograph made to accompany an Army Air Forces report dated 12 July 1946. The relative dihedrals of the wings and the horizontal stabilizers/elevators are composed of different skins. The horizontal stabilizers and the dorsal fin had aluminum-alloy frames with Alclad skins. The rudder, elevators, and ailerons were of aluminum-alloy frames with fabric skins. (NMUSAF)

The flaps are lowered on A-26C-20-DT 43-22502. Each wing had an inboard flap between the fuselage and the engine nacelle and a longer outboard flap. The flaps were constructed of Alclad skin on aluminum-alloy frames. There was an air deflector mounted on the top of the wing immediately to the front of each flap. The flaps and deflectors were operated electrically. (NMUSAF)

A Douglas A-26C wears all-black camouflage with rocket launchers under the wings on 27 October 1947. After World War II, the U.S. Army Air Forces retired its A-20 Havocs, B-25 Mitchells, and B-26 Marauders from frontline service. It retained the A-26B and A-26C for future use in combat. In 1948, the recently renamed U.S. Air Force discontinued its attack category of aircraft and redesignated the A-26s as B-26s since the B-26 Marauders were no longer in use. (National Archives)

FA-26C-25-DT 43-22576 prepares for a mission in 1945. Some A-26Cs were converted to FA-26C nighttime photo-reconnaissance aircraft. These planes were unarmed and could carry a variety of radar and photographic gear. This aircraft has a radome under the fuselage. (National Archives)

The radome of an FA-26C is aft of the bomb bay. A trailing-antenna mount protrudes from the fuselage immediately to the rear of the radome. An escape hatch is open at the top of the former gunner's compartment. (National Archives)

Workers examine an FA-26C with a radome mounted to the rear of the bomb bay. Attached to the underside of the fuselage forward of the tail cone is a fairing with a flattened bottom. Electronics equipment was contained nearby. (National Archives)

The fiberglass radome has been detached from an FA-26C and lies on the floor to allow a view of the antenna for the mapping radar. The ventral gun turret was removed, and its opening modified to accept the fiberglass radome and radar installation. (National Archives)

XA-26F

No matter what the intended role of an aircraft – observation, reconnaissance, fighter, bomber or attack – increased speed is one of the often-desired improvements.

Such was the case with the Invader. When Chevrolet produced the 2,100-horsepower model R-2800-83 engines, plans were immediately made to install these in the A-26.

In April 1945, Douglas got contracts for A-26Bs with the new powerplants. These 750 aircraft became the A-26D while 1,250 of the glass-nosed model were designated as A-26E. The new engines held the promise to increase the Invader's top speed by 80 MPH and retain all the positive attributes of the existing models.

A prototype of each was converted from existing airframes. A-26B 44-34100 became XA-26D 44-34776. The XA-26E was converted from B-26C 44-35563 and retained its original serial number. While the war ended before either model could be produced, the wing installation of six .50-caliber machine guns developed for the A-26D was integrated into ongoing Invader production.

The XA-26F sought to increase speed further. This aircraft, serial number 44-34586, was essentially an XA-26D with four-bladed props rather than three-blade units, and a GE J31 turbojet in the rear fuselage, which exhausted through the tail. The speed combination results did not meet expectations or justify the cost of lost bomb load capacity. This combination precluded further development.

In a quest for an even faster Invader, the staff at Wright Field, Ohio, mated a General Electric I-16 jet engine to A-26B-61-DL 44-34586. The result was the XA-26F prototype. This aircraft retained the two radial engines and the eight-gun general-purpose nose. (NMUSAF)

The XA-26F prototype mounted the General Electric I-16 (later standardized as the J-31) jet engine inside the fuselage to the rear of the wing. A large air scoop on top of the fuselage provided air for the jet engine, whose exhaust was in the tail of the fuselage. (NMUSAF)

The jet intake on top of the fuselage of the XA-26F is clearly visible from this angle. To accommodate the jet engine, accessories, jet intake, and necessary additional fuel stores, designers removed the turrets, gunner's station, and some radio equipment. (NMUSAF)

JD-1

While the U.S. Navy was fond of the work of Invader designer Ed Heinemann – the SBD was one of his designs, and the Naval Air Systems Command later created the Edward H. Heinemann Award for significant contribution to aircraft design – the Navy was not an initial purchaser of the A-26.

In 1945 one A-26B and one A-26C were acquired by the Navy for testing. The two aircraft were designated as XJD-1. "J" was the Navy designation for "utility" aircraft while "D" designated Douglas as the manufacturer. A-26B-DL 44-34217 received Navy Bureau of Aeronautics number (BuNo) 57990 and A-26C-DT 44-35467 became Bureau Number (BuNo) 57991.

After V-J Day on 15 August 1945, a mixture of 150 undelivered RAF and excess USAAF A-26Cs were transferred to the Navy. They became JD-1 Invaders Bureau Numbers 77139 through 77224. In 1947 two ex-RAF A-26Cs, RAF serial numbers KL690 and KL691, which were formerly USAAF 43-22749 and 43-22482 respectively, became Bureau Numbers 80621 and 80622.

More than 50 additional former Army Invaders joined the Navy and became Bureau Numbers 140326 through 140377. In all, seven Navy utility squadrons were equipped with JD-1 Invaders.

As opposed to their combat aircraft design, these squadrons used Invaders as target tugs, drone controllers and general utility aircraft for several years. The introduction of the tri-service designation system in 1962 reclassified the type from JD-1 to UB-26J. The "U" was a "utility" designation of the tri-service unified system.

The U.S. Navy began Invader operations with an ex-Army A-26B and this ex-Army A-26C in 1945. The two initial aircraft were given the designation XJD-1. As more Invaders joined Navy ranks, they were designated JD-1 and were used in non-combat roles. (Stan Piet collection)

U.S. Navy Chief Machinist C.E. Storm ejects from a Douglas JD-1 Invader during ejection seat tests over Naval Auxiliary Air Facility El Centro, California, in 1951. After the RAF's successful test of the new Martin-Baker ejection seat in a Gloster Meteor, the U.S. Navy became interested in the seat. The first successful test was ejected from the rear compartment of a JD-1 near Philadelphia, Pennsylvania, on 1 November 1946. (U.S. Navy National Museum of Naval Aviation)

A U.S. Navy Grumman F9F Panther fighter jet, left, makes a simulated gunnery run on a target sleeve towed by a USN JD-1 over Southern California on 9 July 1951. The target sleeve is the white object about midway between the F9F and the JD-1. (NMUSAF)

A Douglas JD-1 in high-visibility markings functions as a target tug during a flight near Naval Air Station Patuxent River, Maryland on 29 July 1946. The U.S. Navy Bureau Number on the tail is 77216. (NMUSAF)

A Douglas JD-1 flies high above mountainous terrain in March 1949. The plane is coded "UH," which pertained to Utility Squadron 7 (VU-7). The plane's individual number was 2, as marked on the side of the nose and on the right wing.

Douglas JD-1 U.S. Navy Bureau Number (BuNo) 77211 was assigned to Composite Squadron 2 (VC-2) at Quonset Point, Rhode Island. The JD-1s had special noses with clear domes. They lacked turrets but retained the clear enclosure aft of the wings.

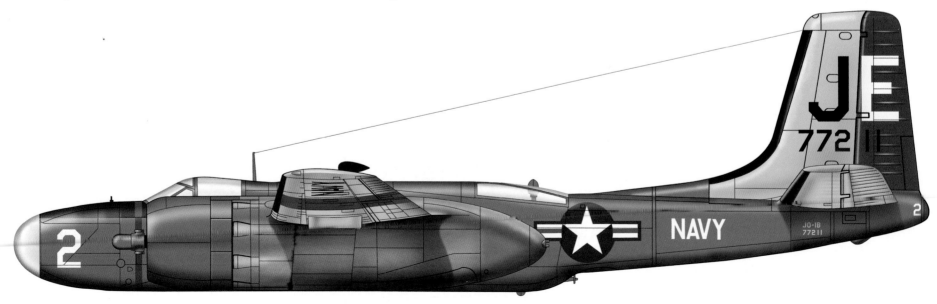

A bomb cart delivers a supply of blue practice bombs to a flightline of A-26s. Crewmen load an A-26B with a six-.50-caliber machine-gun, all-purpose nose and an early-type escape hatch over the right side of the cockpit. Soft covers have been placed over the barrels of the .50-caliber machine guns to protect them from moisture, dust, and foreign objects. There has been considerable wear to the paint of the antiglare panel on the left cowling. (Stan Piet collection)

The first unit to operate the A-26 overseas was the 13th Bomb Squadron, 3rd Bomb Group, Fifth Air Force, known as the Grim Reapers. The unit received four A-26 aircraft on 23 June 1944. Reaper pilots were dismayed to find that the massive engine nacelles and low canopy restricted the cockpit view and made the aircraft inadequate for low level attacks. This was the foremost complaint that led Gen. George Kenney, commander of the Far East Air Forces, to soundly condemn the A-26 with his famous statement, "We do not want the A-26 under any circumstances as a replacement for anything."

A bubble canopy introduction overcame much of the restricted-view issue. Meanwhile, the Army Air Forces was already committed to transition A-20, B-26 and B-25 units to the Invader. Accordingly, the Pacific 319th Bomb Group received A-26s in March 1945.

Meanwhile in the European Theater, and to the relief of many at Douglas and in the procurement branch, the 553d Bomb Squadron, 386th Bomb Group, Ninth Air Force, flew eight evaluation missions with the Invader in late September 1944. Commanders stated the unit was happy to replace its current A-20 and B-25 fleet with new A-26s.

The first to convert was the 416th Bomb Group. It deployed the A-26 on 17 November 1944. The 409th Bomb Group took the Invader to combat in late November. However, A-26C production lagged behind demand. Consequently, A-26Bs followed A-20 lead ships in these groups. This arrangement limited the formation's performance capabilities to the Havoc's capabilities. By the end of the war, the Ninth Air Force had lost 67 Invaders, but flown 11,567 missions and dropped 18,054 tons of bombs.

The Twelfth Air Force in Italy assigned new A-26s to the 47th Bomb Group in January 1945. After WWII, the Army Air Forces executed its plan to replace the A-20 Havoc and B-26 Marauder entirely with A-26 Invaders, although many units still operated the B-25 Mitchell.

Invader A-26B-5-DL 41-39118 sits on a steel mat in Papua New Guinea in June 1944. Several A-26s of the 3rd Bombardment Group performed combat evaluation of the aircraft.

An A-26B-5-DL is parked on a mat in Papua New Guinea in June 1944. It shipped from Oakland, California, in May 1944 and was assembled in Finschhafen, Papua New Guinea.

A-26B-5-DL 41-39116 displays its right side. The tips of the dorsal fin and the rudder were painted a dark color. This plane had two sets of .50-caliber package guns on the underside of each wing.

An A-26B with six .50-caliber machine guns in the nose and two pairs of .50-caliber package guns under each wing takes off from an airfield in Europe in late 1944. Evidence of invasion stripes is visible on the underside of the fuselage aft of the wings. (NMUSAF)

During the last year of World War II, A-26B-15-DL 41-39186 was assigned to the 553rd Bombardment Squadron, 386th Bombardment Group, based at Great Dunmow, England. The plane had the code AN-W and a yellow band with black borders on the tail.

A Douglas A-26B-15-DT of the 386th Bombardment Group banks right during a mission. The tail number is 322343, which equates to USAF serial number 43-22343. The cowlings were blue. (Stan Piet collection)

An A-26 of the 386th Bombardment Group takes off in England in 1944. The nose gear rotates as it is retracted. The retraction swivel allows the wheel to fit in the nose-gear bay. The doors for the nose-gear bay were wider at the rear. (National Archives)

43

An A-26C of the 386th Bombardment Group takes off on a mission. A-26C 41-39199, an A-26C-2-DL, was the fourth to be produced. Only the individual aircraft code, D, from the aircraft/squadron code is visible. (National Archives)

Another A-26 of the 386th Bombardment Group, code AN-K, is viewed from the rear at the group's base in France around the fall of 1944. The code AN pertained to the 553rd Bombardment Squadron.

Douglas Invaders are prepared for missions. They include a B-26C with a blue cowling in the foreground and a plane with the RG fuselage code of the 552nd Bombardment Squadron in the background. Both feature the yellow tail stripe of the 386th Bombardment Group, Ninth Air Force. (Stan Piet collection)

Engines run on Tulsa-built A-26B-15-DT 43-22341 of the 386th Bomb Group at Advanced Air Base A-92 in St.-Trond, Belgium, around the end of World War II. The 386th was based at St.-Trond from 9 April 1945 until July 1945. The cowlings and propeller domes were painted blue. (Stan Piet collection)

A flight crew prepares to board their A-26C at a base in Italy. The A-26C had a hatch in the bottom of the nose for the bombardier's convenience. The man on the ground to the left holds the retractable boarding ladder. Above the flap for the ladder door is a recessed step. The early-style, front-hinged cockpit hatch is present on the cockpit enclosure. (Urban Linn via Stan Piet)

The pilot is in the cockpit of an A-26B in Italy while his copilot and gunner stand on the wing. This plane had the six-machine-gun nose and the improved clamshell-type doors on the canopy. A bead sight is visible to the front of the pilot's side of the windscreen. (Urban Linn via Stan Piet)

At an airfield in Italy during the final months of World War II, A-26C-20-DT 43-22547 of the 47th Bomb Group runs-up its engines. The bombardier is inside the clear nose. The number 52 is on the dorsal fin above the tail number, 3225487. (Urban Linn via Stan Piet)

45

Invaders of the 47th Bombardment Group, such as this A-26B, helped the group win a Distinguished Unit Citation in April 1945. The unit attacked retreating German forces for 60 hours in the Brenner Pass area and prevented the escape of large numbers of the enemy. (Urban Linn via Stan Piet)

Airmen investigate A-26C-25-DT 43-22580 of the 47th Bombardment Group, 97th Bombardment Squadron after it crash-landed at Pisa Airdrome in Italy in the spring of 1945. The plane was painted in overall black camouflage for nighttime interdiction missions. (Urban Linn via Stan Piet)

Douglas A-26C-20-DT 43-22555 was assigned to the 86th Bombardment Squadron, 47th Bombardment Group, based at Grosseto, Italy, in early 1945. On the forward part of the fuselage is the insignia of the 86th Bomb Squadron. The insignia features a wolf in a top hat with a bomb in its hand while hiding behind a cloud at night with the moon and searchlight beams in the distance. (NMUSAF)

A-26C-20-DT 43-22555 parks in Grosseto, Italy. It was painted all black for nighttime interdiction duties. The single, early-style escape hatch is open on the right side of the cockpit. The 86th Bomb Squadron, 47th Bomb Group, was part of the U.S. Twelfth Air Force. (NMUSAF)

An A-26C, code T6-N, of the 573rd Bombardment Squadron, 391st Bombardment Group, Ninth Air Force, flies at low altitude over farmland in the final part of World War II. The plane is in overall bare-aluminum finish with an antiglare panel to the front of the cockpit windscreen. The radio-direction-finder (RDF) "football" antenna is a dark color. The yellow triangle of the 391st Bomb Group is on the tail. (NMUSAF)

The yellow triangle symbol of the 391st Bombardment Group and the P2 code for the 572nd Bombardment Squadron are emblazoned on A-26C-25-DT 43-22653. Two pairs of .50-caliber package guns are visible under the wing. On 23 December 1944 the 391st Bomb Group converted from the B-26 Marauders to the A-26 Invaders in April 1945. The group flew their final mission on 3 May. (Stan Piet collection)

The flight crew of an A-26B prepares to embark on a mission. The early-style escape hatch over the cockpit's right side is open. Black and white invasion wing stripes indicate this aircraft was in the European Theater of Operations (ETO) in mid-1944. (NMUSAF)

An A-26B is in trouble as smoke streams from its right engine nacelle. Flak often was the cause of a downed A-26, although sometimes an enemy fighter would score a kill on one. (NMUSAF)

An A-26B with a six-gun nose and several other A-26s in the distance park at an advanced base of the 409th Bombardment Squadron in Europe in the winter of 1944-45. The 409th was based at Bretigny, France, through most of the winter before it moved to Laon-Couvron Air Base, France, in February 1945. In the foreground near the closest A-26 are several pup tents. Tents were used to shelter ground crewmen from the elements while they worked on the plane and to shelter tools or equipment from rain and snow. (NMUSAF)

Douglas A-26B-35-DL 41-39426 lands at an airfield in Europe. The all-purpose nose is armed with the six-gun configuration of .50-caliber M2 machine guns. Only the letter H of the fuselage code is visible. (NMUSAF)

The A-26s had an early proclivity for landing-gear failures—particularly with the nose gear. This A-26C suffered such a failure and lead to collateral damage of bent propellers. Nose-gear failures problems recurred even into the Vietnam War. (NMUSAF)

49

For Pete's Sake was assigned to the 670th Bombardment Squadron and bore the unit/ aircraft code F6-P. The A-26B was named to honor the pilot's wife. Lt. Wayne Musgrove's wife, Ollie Willie Gray, was nicknamed "Pete" even before birth. (Stan Piet collection)

For Pete's Sake taxis at its home base at Wethersfield, England in 1944. The plane's nickname and related pinup art were painted on the side of the nose. This A-26B completed a total of 46 combat missions by the end of World War II. (Stan Piet collection)

A left-rear view of *For Pete's Sake,* A-26B-15DT 43-22330, shows the plane's squadron/ aircraft code, F6-P. Visible under the left wing are two gun packages. A dark-colored stripe was painted on the rear of the rudder. (Stan Piet collection)

For Pete's Sake, Douglas A-26B-15DT 43-22330 of the 670th Bombardment Squadron, 416th Bombardment Group, Ninth Air Force, runs its engines on a taxiway at Wethersfield, England, in the summer of 1944. (Stan Piet collection)

A long line of A-26s of the 3rd Bombardment Group park near a runway toward the end of World War II. In agreement with the 3rd Bomb Group's practice, each plane has a letter code on the vertical tail and colored bands on the tip of the vertical tail as designated by the squadron. In the Pacific Theater, the 3rd, 41st, and 319th Bombardment Groups were equipped with A-26s. (NMUSAF)

This A-26B's tail markings of are of the 3rd Bombardment Group. The group served with the Fifth Air Force in the Pacific. Three machine guns were installed in each wing during A-26 production. The six wing guns and eight nose guns have dust covers. (NMUSAF)

This 3rd Bombardment Group A-26B-51-DL, 44-3429, crash-landed at an airfield on Okinawa in September 1945. The landing gear, propellers, and the fuselage bottom are damaged. Preparatory to recovery, a hoist sling is attached to the fuselage. (NMUSAF)

An A-26B of the 48th Bombardment Squadron, 41st Bombardment Group, prepares for combat operations on 8 July 1945. This plane has three .50-caliber machine guns in each wing and seven sets of zero-length rocket-launcher stubs under each wing. (National Archives)

The crew of A-26B Short Stuff of the 319th Bombardment Group return from their first raid on the Japanese homeland. They participated in an attack against railroad marshalling yards on Kyushu on 16 July 1945. The crew recently redeployed from the Mediterranean Theater. (National Archives)

Maintenance personnel refuel and service an A-26B assigned to the 12th Bombardment Group, U.S. Tenth Air Force, in India in 1945. A stylized tiger's head was painted on the six-gun nose. Green and yellow bands are to the rear of the nose. (Stan Piet collection)

A 12th Bomb Group A-26B with a tiger's head painted on the all-purpose nose is parked at a base in India. The 12th Bombardment Group received its A-26s in 1945 and trained with these new planes when the war ended that summer. (Stan Piet collection)

Near the end of World War II, formations of Republic P-47 Thunderbolt fighters fly over a base where numerous A-26Cs are parked. Faster fighter jets would quickly eclipse the P-47, but the A-26s would soldier on for several more decades. (National Archives)

An A-26C of the 47th Bombardment Group bears the motto "JOIN THE REGULAR ARMY" on the nose. This slogan was a common refrain in the immediate postwar era. This photo was featured in AAF Review in August 1946. (National Archives)

A-26Cs of the 47th Bombardment Group line up at Lawson Air Force Base, Georgia, on 27 February 1947. The planes were used for an indoctrination course to load 250-pound general-purpose bombs. The second plane is A-26C-55-DT 44-35967. (National Archives)

Ammunition belts for the .50-caliber nose machine guns of an A-26B hang from the gun bay at Biggs Air Force Base, Texas, on 30 April 1947. Underwing 4.5-inch HVARs (high-velocity aircraft rockets) are mounted on zero-length launchers. (National Archives)

In 1948, the newly instituted U.S. Air Force redesignated its A-26s as B-26s. The USAF kept many of these planes on the active rolls and transferred others to the Air National Guard, such as these B-26Cs and B-26Bs of the Arkansas Air National Guard. (NMUSAF)

After World War II, several Douglas B-26s served as test platforms for a type of experimental cargo pod or self-contained pallet that could be dropped at low altitude to resupply troops. The device was fitted with a wheel and two skids. (NMUSAF)

An experimental cargo pod was attached to a bomb shackle, which in turn was fastened to a sway-brace assembly suspended from the wing. The skids were swivel-mounted on struts and had shock absorbers, the upper ends of which fit into openings in the side of the pod. (NMUSAF)

B-26B-45-DL 44-34137, shorn of its wings to eliminate lift, was dubbed the *Wingless Wonder* in 1950 at Air Materiel Command, Wright-Patterson Air Force Base, Ohio. It was used in high-speed brake experiments. The goal was to improve aircraft landing gears. (National Archives)

Korea

After WWII many Invaders were sold as surplus or provided to allied nations. However, the United States did retain many examples, and the type was abundant when the U.S. Air Force became a separate branch on 18 September 1947.

The USAF removed the 'attack' designation when A-26s became B-26s as a result of widespread aircraft redesignations in June 1948. The earlier Martin B-26 was no longer on the roster of USAF aircraft. Consequently, the USAF officials felt there would be no confusion – yet confusion lingers 70 years later.

When war broke out in Korea, the Invader was once again on the front lines. The first offensive action by the U.S. Far East Air Forces was a strike launched with a dozen B-26s against rail yards on 28 June 1950.

These 12 aircraft were a portion of the 26 Fifth Air Force B-26s that were based in Japan. Additional Invaders were added, until the ranks averaged just under 150. Due to maintenance and crew shortages, only about half of that number were available on any given day. Near the war's start, the Invader was utilized as a nighttime ground strike aircraft. It was the best available aircraft for that mission.

Later, the Invaders were based in the Korea peninsula. This location dramatically reduced pilot fatigue and increased aircraft availability. Most of the early Invader missions in Korea were strategic actions, such as bombing and strafing rail yards and supply convoys. Tactical missions also began to be flown as troop concentrations were added to the target list.

B-26s returned to combat in 1950 over Korea. This A-26B of the 3rd Bombardment Group, Far East Air Forces, is parked beside a load of ordnance. Typical Korean War ordnance included napalm canisters, .50-caliber ammo, 4.5-inch HVARs, and small fragmentation bombs. (National Archives)

Douglas B-26B-51-DL 44-34331 of the 3rd Bombardment Group flies a mission over mountainous terrain in Korea. Early in the war, the 3rd Bomb Group staged out of Iwakuni Air Base, Japan. Drop tanks were a necessity for the long flights.

A B-26B with a six-machine-gun nose and armed with three 4.5-inch HVARs under each wing is marked with the buzz number BC-250. The letters BC were assigned to the B-26, and 250 represented the last three digits of the plane's USAF serial number. (NMUSAF)

55

Tech Sgt. Arthur L. Starling and Sgt. J. C. Lovelace fine-tune the installation of a Browning .50-caliber M2 machine gun. The gun was part of a package gun assembly, under the wing of a B-26 Invader of the 3rd Bombardment Group, U.S. Fifth Air Force, in March 1951. (National Archives)

To achieve concentrated, accurate fire from the B-26's fixed machine guns, it was necessary to boresight them periodically. Here, a B-26 pilot boresights the three guns in the left wing while several of his fellow pilots observe the procedure. (National Archives)

Cpl. J. C. Lovelace loads .50-caliber ammunition into the nose bay of a B-26B during the early days of the Korean War. The bay door is held open by a brace at the front. The barrels of the Browning .50-caliber M2 gun barrels are fitted with blast tubes. At the front of the nose is a small hole: this was the opening for the gun camera. (National Archives)

Airman 2nd Class Thomas P. McCurdy, a B-26 gunner with the 3rd Bombardment Group, loads .50-caliber ammunition into the dorsal turret of his plane in October 1952. To reload the guns, it was necessary to remove the dome of the turret. (National Archives)

Flashlights in hand, two armorers check the .50-caliber nose guns and ammo of a B-26B in Korea in April 1952. The word "NEBBA" is visible on the left gun-bay access door. This plane was participated in the 3rd Bomb Wing's 15,000th night sortie. (National Archives)

A Douglas B-26 with a gun nose drops a load of 500-pound general-purpose bombs on a target in a populated area in Korea. Prime targets in such areas included railroad marshaling yards, transportation facilities, supply depots, and military command and infrastructure facilities. (NMUSAF)

Ground crewmen use chocks to secure the wheels of *Brown Nose*, a B-26B of the 731st Bombardment Squadron, 3rd Bombardment Group. The plane was painted overall black; aircraft with such camouflage by then had red identification markings and white bombs were used as mission markings. (Stan Piet collection)

Douglas B-26B-55-DL 44-34429 of the 3rd Bombardment Group in Korea sports black camouflage for nighttime interdiction missions and red trim. Even the hubcaps, the wing-gun covers, and the oil-cooler-intake cover are red. (Stan Piet collection)

Crewmen and dignitaries pose with *Brown Nose* on Marston mat at the 2nd Bombardment Group's base in Korea. Mission markings are plastered over the side of the fuselage and even on the left nose-gear-bay door. (Stan Piet collection)

In Korea, it was common to replace the gun noses on B-26Bs with the bombardier's nose, so the presence of a bombardier's nose is not necessarily proof an aircraft is a B-26C. *The Golden Bear*, B-26B-66-DL 44-34700, in the foreground is one example. (NMUSAF)

Another example of a B-26B with a bombardier's nose was A-26B-55-DL 44-34427. This plane was damaged by a MiG on 9 April 1951 while it served with the 729th Bombardment Squadron, 452nd Bombardment Group. (NMUSAF)

The much-photographed *Brown Nose,* B-26B-55-DL 44-34552, is shown in overall black camouflage for nighttime interdiction missions. "USAF" is painted in large, white letters on the underside of the left wing. (Stan Piet collection)

A clear bombardier's nose has replaced the original all-purpose gun nose on B-26B-55-DL 44-34340 at a base in Korea. The vertical red stripe on the cockpit was a visual warning aid to remind personnel of the spinning propellers' locations. (Stan Piet collection)

No Sweat was the crew nickname for B-26B-55-DL 44-34344. It was another of the B-26Bs transformed with a clear bombardier's nose. The plane was painted overall black, with red markings, and propeller-warning stripe. (Stan Piet collection)

Invader serial number 41-39101 is equipped with a highly modified nose that houses the Bell Labs-developed AN/AAS-1 Airborne Infrared Search and Detection equipment. Project Redbird was a secret effort to incorporate infrared technology into interdiction in 1953. Assigned to the 13th Bomb Squadron, 3rd Bomb Wing, the intent was that on moonless nights the AN/AAS-1 would locate the heat given off by Communist locomotives. This signature allowed the aircraft to mark the target with bombs or rockets while accompanying Invaders attacked the train. Prior to each mission, the nose-mounted sensor was packed with dry ice to cool the rudimentary detection equipment. (Col. Sigmund Alexander via the National Museum of the United States Air Force)

A-26B-30 DL 41-39401 was the only aircraft equipped with this secret experimental equipment. Photographs of the aircraft were officially prohibited. This aircraft, without its unique nose and equipment, survives today at the Fantasy of Flight Museum. (Col. Sigmund Alexander via NMUSAF)

A crewman signals OK from the clear nose of *Monie*, B-26B-61-DL 44-34517, in Pusan, Korea in 1952. The B-26B was assigned to the 37th Bomb Squadron, 17th Bomb Group. *Monie* was the pet name that 1st Lt. Robert Mikesh used for his wife Ramona. Mikesh, the pilot, survived the Korean and Vietnam wars, and later became curator of the Smithsonian's National Air and Space Museum. (NMUSAF)

A crewman sits in *The 7th Chadwick*, B-26B-66-DL 44-34698, while the engines run. *The 7th Chadwick* was flown by Lt. Col. Alvin R. Fortney, commander of the 13th Bomb Squadron, 3rd Bomb Wing. The aircraft was lost on 8 August 1952. 1st Lt. William Holcom, Staff Sgt. Grady Weeks, as well as pilot and major league baseball player Maj. Robert Neighbors, radioed that they must bail out. They were never found. (NMUSAF)

The flight crew of a Douglas B-26B prepare for a mission with the assistance of ground crewmen. This plane has the six-gun nose, three machine guns in each wing, and seven rocket launchers under each wing. In the background is another B-26B. (Stan Piet collection)

High-visibility orange paint and highly polished aluminum characterize this B-26B-66-DL in Air National Guard use. The tail number is preceded by a zero in the style seen on B-26s in the 1950s. This style indicated an aircraft had been produced at least a decade earlier. This tail number translates to USAF serial number 44-34665. (Stan Piet collection)

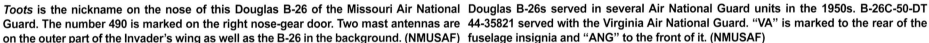

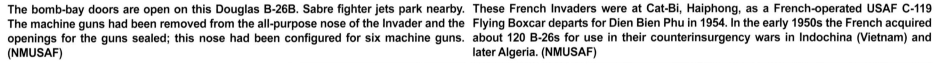

Toots is the nickname on the nose of this Douglas B-26 of the Missouri Air National Guard. The number 490 is marked on the right nose-gear door. Two mast antennas are on the outer part of the Invader's wing as well as the B-26 in the background. (NMUSAF)

Douglas B-26s served in several Air National Guard units in the 1950s. B-26C-50-DT 44-35821 served with the Virginia Air National Guard. "VA" is marked to the rear of the fuselage insignia and "ANG" to the front of it. (NMUSAF)

The bomb-bay doors are open on this Douglas B-26B. Sabre fighter jets park nearby. The machine guns had been removed from the all-purpose nose of the Invader and the openings for the guns sealed; this nose had been configured for six machine guns. (NMUSAF)

These French Invaders were at Cat-Bi, Haiphong, as a French-operated USAF C-119 Flying Boxcar departs for Dien Bien Phu in 1954. In the early 1950s the French acquired about 120 B-26s for use in their counterinsurgency wars in Indochina (Vietnam) and later Algeria. (NMUSAF)

A B-26B with a six-gun nose, flies low over rice paddies in Vietnam in 1963. The United States sent small numbers of B-26Bs and reconnaissance RB-26s to South Vietnam in the early 1960s. In the days before full-fledged American involvement in the area, these planes were flown covertly. They had South Vietnamese markings and observers on board but were flown by American "advisors." Twelve B-26s were in the country by 1963. (National Archives)

A B-26B with an eight-gun nose is parked at Bien Hoa Air Base, South Vietnam, in July 1962. Technically it was assigned to the South Vietnam Air Force. It is armed with a rocket pod and two napalm bombs under each wing. There are no machine guns in the wings. (National Archives)

A South Vietnam Air Force B-26B with a six-gun nose and an unusual horizontal antenna under the rear of the fuselage was photographed from a plane rigged to spray defoliants. The VNAF insignia was similar to the USAF version, but with a red border and bars. (National Archives)

This A-26B wears the yellow, red and blue markings of Không lực Việt Nam Cộng hòa – KLVNCH, or South Vietnam Air Force. In October 1961 a detachment of the 4400th Combat Crew Training Squadron was sent to Vietnam as part of Operation Farm Gate. The mission was to ostensibly train Vietnamese crews in the operation of the Invader.

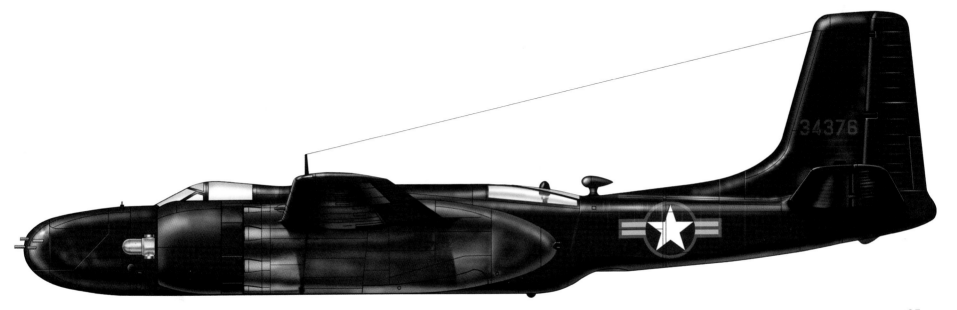

B-26K 64-17640, the first production aircraft of the series, is parked at Edwards Air Force Base, California, in June 1964. The B-26K Counter-Invader first flew on 26 May 1964. The U.S. Air Force took delivery of these planes from June 1964 to April 1965. Most of the B-26Ks were initially assigned to the 602nd Fighter Squadron (Commando) at Hurlburt Air Force Base. The final seven planes were sent to the 605th Air Commando Squadron in the Panama Canal Zone. (National Archives)

After the Korean cease fire, the next combat use of American Invaders was the ill-fated Bay of Pigs operation in Cuba. For this operation, 15 USAF Invaders were painted in Cuban Air Force markings. One was flown to Miami on 15 April 1961 as a faux defection, and the others were used to strike against targets in Cuba. These missions were flown by Cuban expatriate pilots on 15-17 April. On 18 April 1961, Americans manned the planes over water, but not inland to avoid capture. Several were shot down.

On the other side of the world, the Invader saw combat almost continuously. In 1951 the United States provided the French with 38 B-26s for use in Indochina. However, the demands of the Korean war precluded more such transfers until 1954. Then, 16 more were loaned from the Far East Air Force at Clark Air Base. Eventually these loaners were replaced by more Invaders provided by the Mutual Defense Assistance Program.

The Geneva Accord split Vietnam into the Communist North Vietnam and the French - and later U.S.-backed - South Vietnam in October 1954. The last French forces left Vietnam on 28 April 1956. A part of the Accord prohibited jet combat aircraft in the region.

In 1961, 16 unmarked B-26s were sent to Thailand as part of Operation Mill Pond. It was an effort to halt communist incursions in the Laotian Civil War. The aircraft were maintained as Air America aircraft, an airline owned by the CIA. The debacle of the similar Bay of Pigs operation caused the cancellation of Mill Pond after the initial training operations.

In April 1961 the U.S. Air Force began to prepare a counterinsurgency force. To do so, the 4400th Combat Crew Training Squadron was formed at Eglin Air Force Base, Florida, with the responsibility of training Vietnamese in the use of the B-26, C-47 and

T-28. The operation was dubbed Jungle Jim. In October 1961 a detachment of this unit was sent to Vietnam in Operation Farm Gate. This detachment was renamed as the 1st Air Commando Wing on 8 July 1963. Among the aircraft sent in this operation were four B-26 Invaders. The Invaders arrived at Bien Hoa in December.

Farm Gate missions initially required the presence of at least one South Vietnamese, who the Americans were ostensibly 'training,' in the aircraft. Following the 2 August 1964 Gulf of Tonkin incident, there was no longer a requirement for a Vietnamese to be on the aircraft.

The presence of Americans in air combat over Vietnam became very apparent on 3 February 1963 when a Farm Gate RB-26 was shot down and killed captains John Shaughnessy and John Bartley.

A wing failure on a B-26 during a 16 August 1963 combat mission cost the lives of two more Americans as well as a Vietnamese. The incident was followed by a similar failure in Florida in February 1964. These failures led to the creation of the final Invader variant.

On Mark Engineering, engaged in civilian transport conversions of Invaders, had been licensed by Douglas for some time as the exclusive producer of Invader parts. It is not surprising that the Air Force turned to the firm to create an Invader with strengthened wings.

Dubbed the Counter Invader, and initially designated B-26K, the aircraft was a significant improvement. The rebuilds were so extensive that the aircraft were given new serial numbers in the range 64-17640 through 64-17679. Because Thailand prohibited bombers from being station in that country, in May 1966 the Invader regained its old attack designation, and the B-26K was reclassified as the A-26A.

The first production B-26K carries a different load of underwing stores in August 1964. It carried two drop tanks on the inboard pylons and six napalm canisters. The wing pylons could hold up to 8,000 pounds in weapons and stores. For the counterinsurgency role, the favored weapons were napalm, rocket pods, and cluster bombs. The VHF-101 short-range two-way radio antenna protrudes from the top of the fuselage directly above the propeller hub. (National Archives)

B-26K 64-17640, the first of its series, is seen from the left side at Edwards Air Force Base, California, in June 1964. Underwing stores on each side consist of (from inboard to outboard) one pylon drop tank, one B-11 napalm bomb, and two LAU-3A rocket pods. Each LAU-3A pod contained 19 2.75-inch folding-fin-stabilized rockets. The pods had jettisonable nose and tail cones to reduce drag until the moment rockets are fired. (National Archives)

The first production B-26K, B-26K 64-17640, parks at Edwards Air Force Base, California, on 10 August 1964. Initially, these planes were painted a glossy green on the upper surfaces and sides and a glossy light gray on the lower surfaces and sides. There was a straight, hard demarcation line between the two colors. The tail number was a light gray or white. The tail cones of the nacelles were black. Various communications antennas were on the top of the fuselage. (National Archives)

Six napalm canisters and two drop tanks are on the wing pylons of the first B-26K at Edwards Air Force Base on 10 August 1964. The 165-gallon wingtip tanks gave these planes the extended flight time that was an advantage in counter-insurgency operations. These missions often it took hours of loitering to get an advantage over the enemy. Pylon-mounted drop tanks gave the B-26K even more range and loiter time over potential targets. (National Archives)

For the evaluations of the first B-26K at Edwards Air Force Base in August 1964, a test probe was mounted on the right wing. The probe is visible to the left of the wingtip fuel tank. Spotlights are mounted on the nacelle tail cones. (National Archives)

A navigation light is on each side of the wingtip fuel tanks. It is on the demarcation line between the upper and the lower colors. The pointed propeller spinners used on the prototype YB-26K were not installed on the production B-26Ks. (National Archives)

The first production B-26K carryies an underwing load of two drop tanks and six napalm canisters at Edwards Air Force Base on 10 August 1964. Whereas the prototype YB-26K had Pratt & Whitney R-2800-103W engines, the production B-26Ks were powered by the Pratt & Whitney R-2800-52W engines. Hamilton Standard automatic-feathering, fully-reversible propellers were used.

The prototype YB-26K runs up its engines prior to takeoff. It was used in experiments with jet-assisted takeoff (JATO) equipment at Tactical Air Command's Special Air Warfare Center at Hurlburt Field, Florida, in the 1960s. (National Archives)

The JATO-equipped YB-26K takes off from Hurlburt Field. The JATO pod was installed on the bottom of the fuselage aft of the bomb bay. Jet-assisted takeoff allowed heavily loaded aircraft to use shorter-than-normal runways during takeoff. (National Archives)

B-26K (A-26A)

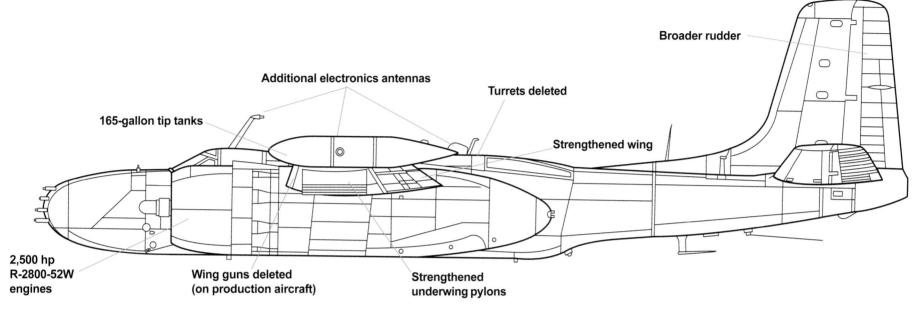

Additional electronics antennas

Turrets deleted

Broader rudder

165-gallon tip tanks

Strengthened wing

2,500 hp
R-2800-52W
engines

Wing guns deleted
(on production aircraft)

Strengthened
underwing pylons

The first A-26K makes a test flight from Edwards Air Force Base in 1964 with a load of drop tanks and napalm canisters. The A-26K featured a wider rudder than previous A-26s. If the aircraft had to be flown on one engine, it handled better with a wider rudder. (National Archives)

A-26K 64-17640, Douglas' first example, flies high above the Southern California desert near Edwards Air Force Base in 1964. In addition to the antennas on top of the fuselage, the A-26Ks had various antennas under the fuselage. Wings were strengthened for support and an ability to carry additional weapons and fuel. (National Archives)

B-26Bs are converted to B-26K Counter-Invaders by On Mark Engineering Company, based at the Van Nuys Airport in California, in the 1960s. The process starts when certain components are stripped from B-26s. On Mark built a reputation by converting surplus B-26 Invaders into executive transport planes. It made both the Marketeer with an unpressurized fuselage and the Marksman with a pressurized fuselage. Consequently, the company was an obvious selection to convert low-use B-26s to B-26Ks. (NMUSAF)

B-26 wings are rebuilt with steel reinforcement strips added to the tops and bottoms of the spars. Wing failure became a serious problem with B-26s that served in Vietnam in the early 1960s. The B-26Ks were expected to carry far greater external stores. Reinforced wings were an initial requirement of the B-26K Counter-Invaders. (NMUSAF)

Fuselages are aligned at the On Mark Engineering plant during conversion to B-26Ks. The nose sections have been removed. The B-26Ks would be issued with solid noses. Each had eight .50-caliber machine guns, but retained the option to install a bombardier's nose. (NMUSAF)

A left wing is rebuilt for a Douglas B-26K Counter-Invader. Heavy-duty wooden stands support the wing assembly. In the foreground is the partially-disassembled engine nacelle. A trouble light hangs from the front wing spar. (NMUSAF)

Workers convert a B-26K. The Hamilton Standard wide-chord propellers and the engines have been installed. The eight-gun nose has been mounted, and antennas have been installed on the top of the fuselage. (NMUSAF)

Personnel load equipment into the bomb bay of a B-26K. The rears of the empennage and nacelles are visible. The spotlights on the tail cones of the YB-26B nacelles are no longer present. (NMUSAF)

Two crewmen service the reconnaissance-camera package in a B-26K modified to RB-26K standards. The man under the bomb bay has one of the reconnaissance cameras on the ground. On the side of the fuselage aft of the bomb bay is an emergency hatch for the camera operator. (NMUSAF)

Air Force personnel inspect a B-26K. Two napalm canisters are mounted on the pylons. Napalm had been around since World War II. Essentially it was jellied gasoline which combusted and spread in all directions when detonated. It was used heavily in Vietnam. (NMUSAF)

An RB-26K of the 1st Air Commando Wing based at Hurlburt Air Force Base, Florida, visits a base in Germany in 1966. RB-26K 17669 started as A-26B-61-DL 44-34606. This Counter-Invader arrived in Southeast Asia in 1966. (NMUSAF)

In May 1967, for political purposes related to the bombers based in Thailand, the B-26Ks were redesignated as A-26A attack aircraft. B-26K 64-17671, with a TA tail code, began service with the 609th Special Operations Squadron based at Nakhon Phanom Royal Thai Air Force Base in 1967. It operated in the covert war against the Pathet Lao and the North Vietnamese in Laos. The plane is painted in Southeast Asia camouflage. The camouflage scheme consists of dark green, medium green, and tan over black. After it returned to the United States, this B-26K was displayed at Florence, South Carolina from 1973 until 1997. It was dismantled for parts in 1998. (NMUSAF)

An A-26A parks on a metal mat at an air base. Small plugs are inserted in the blast tubes of the eight .50-caliber machine guns. The number 675 on the nose-gear door is the last three digits of the serial number 64-17675. (NMUSAF)

The IF tail code of the 603rd Special Operations Squadron is on the tail of A-26A 64-17655, which is painted in Southeast Asia camouflage. Later this plane was placed in storage and eventually disintegrated at Davis-Monthan Air Force Base, Arizona. (NMUSAF)

On Mark Engineering converted Douglas A-26C-40-DT 44-35634 into A-26A 64-17670 in Southeast Asia camouflage. The tail code TA on the adjacent A-26A pertained to the 609th Special Operations Squadron at Nakhon Phanom. (NMUSAF)

A-26A 64-17654 was assigned to the 609th Special Operations Squadron at Nakhon Phanom Royal Thai Air Force Base, Thailand, in the late 1960s. Because of the covert nature of their missions over Laos, these planes did not carry USAF insignia. (NMUSAF)

Douglas RB-26K 64-17643 was converted from A-26C-35-DT 44-35392. The bombardier's nose and the openings in the bomb-bay door for cameras are visible. The plane is in its original gloss green over light gray paint. (NMUSAF)

Personnel service a Douglas A-26A. The eight .50-caliber machine guns in the nose and variety of underwing stores available made the A-26A a highly-effective interdictor of enemy supply-truck traffic in Laos and Vietnam. (NMUSAF)

The access ladder of an A-26A is deployed on the side of the fuselage adjacent to the cockpit. An air scoop is located to the front of the door for the access ladder. The aircraft is parked beside A-26A 64-17677. (NMUSAF)

Douglas A-26A Counter-Invaders are lined up at an air base. No USAF insignia are visible on the planes. Lack of insignia indicates they are located at Nakhon Phanom Royal Thai Air Force Base during the covert deployment to Southeast Asia in the 1960s. (NMUSAF)

Two B-26Ks in the original green-over-gray camouflage scheme fly a training mission over a coastal area in the 1960s. USAF serial number 64-17665 is in the foreground, and 64-17664 is in the background. In May 1966, Detachment 1, 603rd Air Commando Squadron, England AFB Louisiana was deployed to Nakhon Phanom Royal Thai Air Base. There, they were attached to the 606th Air Commando Squadron and redesignated as A-26As. Both A-26As were reassigned to the 634th Combat Support Group at Nakhon Phanom in December 1966. They were later assigned to the 609th Air Commando Squadron in April 1967. (NMUSAF)

At least eight A-26As are on this flightline, presumably at Nakhon Phanom Royal Thai Air Force Base, in the late 1960s. A subdued bat illustration is on the fuselage of the first plane. The second plane is fully loaded with bombs and napalm. (NMUSAF)

Three Douglas A-26A Counter-Invaders rest at an unidentified air base. They lack tail codes and national insignia. The tail numbers are painted in small, white numerals. The planes are painted in Southeast Asia camouflage with black lower surfaces. (NMUSAF)

Douglas A-26A 64-17650 prepares for takeoff on a steel mat runway. This plane was shot down during combat over Southeast Asia on 28 June 1966 with the loss of the crew. It was the first 603rd ACS plane to be lost in combat. (NMUSAF)

B-26K 64-17655 flies over the Caribbean while based in the Panama Canal Zone in the mid-1960s. A bombardier's nose is installed as a possible mount for a reconnaissance camera package. It wears the original green and gray camouflage.

The Douglas A-26As were retired from combat in 1969. The retirement marked the end of a service career that spanned a quarter of a century and three American wars, which included World War II, Korea and Vietnam. Although some of these planes met their ends in combat and accidents, many survive. One survivor is A-26A 64-17651, *Mighty Mouse*, which is preserved in an aerospace museum in South Korea. (NMUSAF)